A COLLECTION OF DREAMSCAPES

Praises for *A Collection of Dreamscapes*

"I hadn't thought it possible for Sng to improve on *A Collection of Nightmares*. I was wrong. In *Dreamscapes*, Sng shatters traditional storytelling and showcases her versatility as a master poet. Tackling odysseys, fairy tales, myths, monsters, and unspeakable violence, she wields words like 'a scythe making graceful strokes', paring her verse to sinew and bone. Not a word is out of place in this ground-breaking collection."—Lee Murray, award-winning author of *Into the Mist*

"I loved this collection of poems that flow in a story cycle; tendrils of images from one flavoring the next. New and old myths, reborn in Sng's brilliant imagination into unique, grownup versions where empowerment rules and old-fashioned revenge is very satisfying."—Linda D. Addison, award-winning author of *How to Recognize a Demon Has Become Your Friend* and HWA Lifetime Achievement Award winner

"Christina Sng uses words to paint landscapes of the realms of mythology, fairy tales, monsters, inner demons, and more. As you travel this exhibition, be prepared to be pulled inside these haunting dreamscapes from humanity's collective unconscious. Don't be surprised if these works begin to haunt your own dreams. This is poetry at its best."—David Lee Summers, author of *The Astronomer's Crypt* and *Owl Dance*

"Outrage howls against human cruelty from verse after verse throughout…This new book overflows with nightmare fodder. Just as importantly, it burns white hot with catharsis. Warriors rage against oppressors, women and girls purge their abusers, and the innocent make necessary transformations into monsters to bring about 'Wrongs made right for once / In this unjust world.' Even as you shudder, you'll smile in empathy and 'enjoy the bloodbath.'"—Mike Allen, World Fantasy Award-nominated author of *Unseaming* and *Aftermath of an Industrial Accident*

"Like a lullaby distorted into a scream, Sng's evocative language sets up beautiful scenes that soon lead the reader deeper and deeper into darkness. Between dreams, myths, fairy tales, and more, readers will find themselves spun into a mystical web of stories that unfold through each finely crafted poem. Sng offers up such a rich world through the different sections, yet the storytelling and vibrancy in each blend seamlessly together. A captivating collection that is not to be missed!"—Sara Tantlinger, Bram Stoker Award-winning author of *The Devil's Dreamland*

"…a journey of monstrous possibilities, surreal surroundings, and entrancing mythologies, and one that—though we all must wake up eventually—I did not want to end."
—Christa Carmen, author of *Something Borrowed, Something Blood-Soaked*

A COLLECTION OF
DREAMSCAPES

BY CHRISTINA SNG

RAW DOG
SCREAMING
PRESS

A Collection of Dreamscapes © 2020 by Christina Sng

Published by Raw Dog Screaming Press
Bowie, MD

First Edition

Cover art: Steven Archer
Book design: Jennifer Barnes
Editor: Stephanie M. Wytovich

Printed in the United States of America
ISBN: 9781947879171
Library of Congress Control Number: 2020931561

www.RawDogScreaming.com

Also by Christina Sng

For my children, may your dreams always be sweet.

TABLE OF CONTENTS

THE LOVE SONG OF ALLEGRA

ALLEGRA

Her name soothes
The mighty beast, enthralled
By her ethereal song.

A tale
Extending far beyond
Our collective memories,

A relic of echoes
Unbound by the years
And retold

By Allegra,
The protagonist
Of songs.

❭

It began with love,
Of Prometheus and
Allegra, his love.

They danced through time,
Entwined in a symphony
Of fire and ice,

Swirling amid
The ancient stars
They called by name.

They were there
At their christening,
At the birth of the world;

Our universe,
Their interstellar playground.
And Allegra sang,

Her song stirred
The heart of life
Into bloom,

Planting barren planets
And moons with
Seeds from her hands.

Prometheus, jealous
Of Allegra's passion,
Returned to raze the land.

Ignited, his fires burned,
Annihilating flourishing worlds
Allegra had sung to birth.

And Allegra,
In silence and grief,
Departed from him,

Fell to Earth,
With whom
She fell in love,

And sang,
Stirring
The muted land.

For Prometheus,
She built a pyre, a promise
To spare Earth his fire.

And for a million years
Life sprang up, painted
In incandescent colors.

Her hands shed corpuscles.
She'd been clawing the soil.
And Allegra,

Exhausted,
Fell into eternal sleep,
Enveloped

In the red and green
Flowers and leaves
She'd beckoned awake.

❭

The cycles pass
In a harried frenzy.
But her song

Endures the twisted
Passage of time.
It is our voice

That echoes it.
A plea to the fire bearer,
To him who destroys peace.

And again,
The symphony of ice
Quenches the flame.

Prometheus, redirected,
Leaves us
Untouched again.

A BAPTISM IN THE LAND OF ALLEGRA

Her skin drank hungrily
As he smeared a paste of blood
And marrow all over her body.

Then he washed her
Tenderly with milk, and after,
Immersed her in rosewater.

Her flesh gleamed
With the glow of many
Succulent young bodies,

Those who had previously loved
And served the ousted queen
And all of her kin.

As he dried her
With the skins
Of the newly dead,

She clasped his hands
Into her fists,
Drawing him

Into her arms
And baptized him in turn
With her love.

Later, he guided her
Into the palace of winds,
Before his frightened people,

Stung
And beaten by war.
They recognized her

And gasped in terror
As their king pronounced her
The new queen of Allegra.

AS CHILDREN

In the forest we grew up
From androgynous children
To blessed adults.

I was the dark angel:
Brown eyes flooded with light,
My raven-black hair

Fanning
In the billowing wind.
The fairies of those days

Caught on
To loose strands of my hair,
Hanging on, giggling

As I twirled,
Arms outstretched
Like an aerial roundabout.

How you applauded in delight.
Those days, the love shone
Transparently from your eyes.

Now they are shielded.
She has put them there
To keep the darkness inside.

You obey in blindness,
Eyes glazed as you crack the whip
Across my naked back,

Once,
Twice,
Fifty times.

I bite my lip, refusing
To lend an accompaniment
To her unending shrieks of laughter.

CELL

She sits beside me,
Tending to my wounds.
I wonder what cause

Would send her,
Such an old woman
To this desolate prison cell.

She weeps over me,
Tears falling
Into my chest wound,

Mixing
With the scorched blood
And shattered ribs inside.

Through the fog
Of blinding pain,
I slowly recognize her,

Softly whisper her name
As others had
In the olden days.

She tells me to hold on to life,
That betrayal is not an end,
But a beginning.

I close my eyes
And see images of deserts
And seaside villages,

A diamond spear
On a thick stone altar,
Above it, a black aurora,

A young girl
With hair of fire and skin of ice
Dancing in the forest.

And I,
At peace,
In the palace of winds.

Myths.
Or a glimpse of the future?
I was all but dead

When they brought me here.
Now I sleep.
Now I dream.

She is gone
When I awake,
The sun in my face

As I wonder
If I had imagined it all
In my mad delirium.

Then I realize
There is no more pain.
No torn flesh,

No recently borne scars
Where once a gaping hole
Divided my heart and my stomach.

Slowly, I crawl to the prison bars.
The guards are busy gambling
Over a frightened young girl.

Swiftly,
I unclasp the bloodspar
From my boot,

Using the sharp end
Of the folded spear
To pick the lock.

I draw the weapon
To its full length, step forth
And make my move.

THE WARRIOR MEPHALA

Mephala kneels before
The statue of Allegra,
Hands clasped like a Buddha,
Heart serene as a whirlwind.

It was here
Where she and her king
Bowed and exchanged
Vows of eternity

Before the goddess
Of love and fertility
All those seasons ago
When she promised

Never again to take
Another innocent soul,
Destroying the warrior in her
For a life of peace and tranquility

Long before
The ground opened
And released hell
To her people

Massacring the elders
With their demonic magic,
Stealing away the weak
To do their bidding.

As the sky fades into darkness,
Mephala casts away her humanity,
Clasps her bloodspar
And leaves to prepare for war.

THE SACRED SPEAR

Mephala runs,
Sacred Spear
Strapped onto her back,
Her heart rattling the bars
Of her ribcage, threatening
To break out screaming.

Her legs are stretched to their limits
But she cannot stop. They move
On their own accord—on instinct.
She feels scorched tears
Burn her tired face—she has not
Known such fear till today.

Behind her, the black aurora follows,
Thick as a tree marrow,
Ravenous for warrior flesh,
Especially this one,
Who stole the diamond spear
It swore to protect.

It trails her scent
For eleven eves
Over the dead sea and sand.
It will not stop until
The warrior is digested in its belly
And melded with its body.

Mephala finally falters
Near the Oracle Valley,
Where the Sacred Cove lies
To charge the Spear's power
And reveal to its bearer
Where the new queen resides.

She bursts into a run
As the cove yawns its presence.

The Guardian of the Spear
Hovers over the horizon,
Nearly spotting her, its olfactories
Tuned to her scent.

Mephala unties the Spear
And hurriedly places it
Onto the stone altar.
Collapsing against the cove wall,
She waits impatiently for
Something miraculous to happen.

The slight hiss outside is familiar—
Mephala hastily crawls
Behind the altar,
Placing her hand on the Spear,
Hoping
Its power will protect her.

The Guardian glides into the cove,
A dark cloud of sawdust
Blocking out the sunlight.
It stops above the stone altar
In the center of the ancient shelter,
Snaking around it, searching.

But the scent is gone.
The winds have carried it
Along with them,
Taken it past the seas
And the mountains
Into a land forgotten.

The Guardian darts outside,
Struggling to find
What it realizes
It has already lost.
Defeated, it leaves the cove
In a mist of dust.

Mephala curls beside the Spear,
Holds it close and falls to rest
As the moon and stars
Realign
For many days
And many nights.

When the warrior finally awakes,
Refreshed, strength injected,
She returns home, armed
With the charged Sacred Spear
And a new quest to find
The daughter of fire and ice.

THE CHILD WHO WOULD BE QUEEN

On all Hallows Eve,
The warrior Mephala
Visits the tiny village of Mer
Where the sea folk
Celebrate the sacred day
With great feasting and prayer.

A young girl,
No more than fifteen
Slips away from the celebrants,
Satchel slung over her shoulder,
Her luminous eyes gleaming
With excitement and adventure.

Free from the clearing,
She flings back her flame-red hair
And hums a low tune,
Summoning a menagerie
Of curious animals
Out from their forest homes.

She greets the birds
With a string of happy chirps,
Hops along gaily with two young rabbits.
She races up a tree with a pair of squirrels
And prances along with a small fawn,
Singing a song about freedom without fear.

Mephala crouches close by,
Amused at the sight before her.
The child certainly has a gift.
But how it fits
Into the grand plan,
She does not comprehend.

Mephala reveals herself to Margritte,
Who freezes, in surprise.

Quickly regaining her composure,
Margritte studies the warrior
And decides she is in no danger.
"What do you want?" she asks.

Mephala takes the Sacred Spear
And kneels before the young girl,
Introducing herself,
"I am Mephala, warrior of Allegra.
And you are our true queen,
The one who will save the world."

Margritte of Mer laughs out loud.
"I am a peasant girl, savage and wild.
What good am I in controlling a crowd?"
Since words cannot explain her role,
Mephala touches the tip of the Sacred Spear
To the heart of the disbelieving girl.

She turns ice-white, eyes wide,
Then bloody with amber fire.
Margritte screams in outrage
But quietens when she feels no pain.
Instead, a serenity washes over her
Like a blessing and a cleansing

As she falls to her knees in tears
And a dark understanding.
"All that I saw, all that horror,
Can be changed by the force of my power?"
Mephala nods. "Your power,
And that of the Sacred Spear."

Margritte of Mer stands,
Wipes the tears from her determined face,
Changed in an instant
From a child's to a queen's.
"Let us go," she says. "There is
Much to learn and much to prepare."

MARGRITTE OF MER

O she is beautiful,
With long flaming hair
That falls down her back
Like a raging waterfall.

"Who is she?" the people ask
In anxious whispers.
"She is Margritte of Mer,"
They say.

"She is the daughter
Of fire and ice,
The one who will bring
The world into reunification.

She is protected
By the great warrior
Mephala, who holds
The Sacred Spear."

The reunification
Will occur,
And the time
Draws near.

WAR AND PEACE

The warrior Mephala
Steps onto the battlefield
Amidst the chaos around her
And fights for peace.

The queen Margritte
Sits by the bed
Of a wounded soldier,
Praying for peace.

Deaths occur
Once every ten seconds;
Life is cheap
In times of war.

THE WAR OF THE FALL

What was love
In war time
But a comfort,
For any moment
Could be our last.

That was when
The warrior Mephala
Met her true love
On the battlefield
In the War of the Fall,

Humans against demons,
Summoned by the demon
Queen herself, who stole
Mephala's king and now
Wore her crown as queen.

But she did not have
The warrior's army.
So she summoned her own
Through a dark portal,
A mile tall and a mile long,

Opening a vast gateway
Into the netherworld
From which monsters bled
Into the lush green plains,
Turning them crimson.

Her people fled in terror.
Only the brave remained
To meet the demon army
Alongside their true queen,
The warrior Mephala

Who led them against
The demons that tore
Everything apart.
"Go for their heads,"

She commanded

And she charged ahead,
Decapitating a trail of
Demons behind her.
Her warriors followed
In her ferocious wake.

Mephala found herself
Flanked by twelve demons,
Scythes in their hands,
Slashing her without hesitation
Across her chest and her back.

She fell, twisting her body
To slice open their necks
Before leaping back up,
Adrenaline numbing the pain,
Taking them all down

Before she reached the ones
Holding the portal open,
Chanting a mystical spell.
She cut them in half with
A swing of the Sacred Spear.

And just like that,
The battle was over.
But a queen does not leave
Her injured warriors
On the battlefield,

Not even when blood pours
Out of her wounds like a river.
She tended to each fallen one
In place of their mothers,
Comforting the dying,

Thanking them
For their courage
Before she herself
Stumbled and paled
From her blood loss.

Then out of the mist,
One of them spoke,
"My Queen,
Let me take care of them."
She turned to see a man

With a strong battle-worn face
And demon blood on his armor,
His eyes were clear as the winter sky,
His hand firmly on his hammer.
"Who are you?" she asked,

Priding herself on knowing
All of her warriors.
He smiled.
"We once played as children,
But I have long since moved

To the north with my family
Where we have been
Guarding the volatile border."
Mephala remembered.
She clasped his hand.

"I recall, old friend."
They were older
But their eyes had not changed.
Kindness and love
Still shone through,

An innocence,
Once treasured,
Now regained,
Even if it was for
But a moment.

This bond, restored,
Soon would be as strong
As the will of the gods.
They would need it
For the war ahead.

THE FINAL BATTLE

We fight,
One battle after another,
Almost impossible
To meet magic with might.

The border of the palace,
Unable to be breached
Till the warrior Mephala
Draws her enemy out instead.

The powerful have their pride,
So she mocks the demon queen
For her cowardice,
Hiding behind her magic.

Words carry and the demon
Flays more, opening up
Another portal in the west
As Mephala waits by her door.

The warrior must send her love
To defend that border instead.
He is strong and brave,
A true commander with honor,

Unlike her king who has become
A sycophant to the demon,
Casting Mephala out to die
When she stole her place as queen.

Over and over,
Mephala mocks the demon,
Till her pride can no longer bear
The scornful stares of her minions.

She comes out to meet
The warrior in battle,

Decked out in armor
As Mephala draws her Spear.

When she sees her slain beasts
Scattered all over the land,
The cowardly demon flees
Back into the castle,

Its drawbridge left open.
Mephala follows,
Along with her warriors,
Ready to end this battle,

Ready to win the war.

MERCY

Mephala charges ahead
With the Sacred Spear,
Freshly sharpened,
Aimed at the heart of her enemy.

She runs across the castle grounds
And spies the demon queen racing,
Elixir of life clutched in her hand,
Into the throne room.

She follows without hesitation,
Brandishing the Spear,
Ready to strike, if the demon
Retaliates with a surprise attack.

She corners her in an alcove
And watches her raise her sword.
But the demon is an alchemist, not a warrior.
Mephala knocks the weapon out of her hand.

She spews poison from her lips
But Mephala knows of her ways,
Swiftly dodging, she narrowly escapes
Losing half her face to acid.

Without a moment's hesitation,
Mephala presses the Spear
Against the demon's face,
Its cold tip touching her skin.

She shivers. The battle is over.
But the demon is not done fighting.
Now the persuasion begins.
"I have wronged you, warrior," she says,

Without an ounce of remorse in her face.
"But my people need their queen,
So I ask you for their sake,
To spare my life."

Mephala almost laughs aloud.
"Your people?" she replies incredulously.
"The same people from whom you stole,
Made slaves of, and slaughtered for sport?"

The demon flinches but holds her head high.
"This isn't about the people, is it?
This is about your king leaving you for me.
What man would choose a warrior over a queen?"

Mephala smiles knowingly.
"Only a foolish man," she states.
"A weak man who is not a warrior,
But a mere sycophant in your court."

"Yes," the demon says haughtily.
"And he belongs to me now."
"He belongs to the worms," Mephala intervenes.
"His heart and entrails are in their stomachs now."

The demon trembles with fear,
But Mephala knows it is just theater.
"Show me mercy, I beg of you," she pleads.
"For the love of the people, spare me my life!"

"I am showing great mercy," Mephala says.
"But mercy to those from whom
You will steal, enslave, and slaughter.
Freeing you will be an act of extreme cruelty.

It will be a cold and merciless act
To my people to let you live.
But your death will bring great joy
And freedom for them."

A genuine tear rolls down the demon's cheek
As Mephala cuts off her head,
Showing her foe great mercy
By giving her a quick death.

THE KING WHO BECAME A SYCOPHANT

"A sycophant becomes a king
As easily as a king becomes a sycophant.
Is that so difficult to conceive?"

Mephala lets the words
Of her queen immerse
As she rises to her feet.

"Lovers switch loyalties
As treacherously as traitors.
Should they not suffer the same punishment?"

Queen Margritte nods,
Her eyes dark.
"Let it be so."

Mephala takes the king
Who became a sycophant
To the place where traitors are punished,

The dank lingering scent
Of fear and death thick in its walls,
The curved marble ceiling

Of the Cave of Sacrifice
Etched with the tales of traitors,
Blood spatters stained into the stone.

She lays him flat
On the cold, sacrificial block,
And straps him in with wolfgut.

His eyes plead for mercy,
His severed voice, begging,
Making incoherent noises.

With great contempt,

She'd crushed his larynx
During the capture.

Her eyes are frost-cold,
Voice wavering,
But only for a second.

"You have committed treason
Against your queen and your state.
You will die twice a traitor's death."

His eyes bulge.
His mouth emits a strangled cry.
Of weak apology or anguish,

Mephala does not know or care.
She plucks his nails out
Like errant weeds.

With a shaven chopper,
Removes his fingers
From their reluctant sockets,

His eyelids cut in a half-moon
To ensure he witnesses every moment
Leading to his death.

She begins with his toenails,
Then his toes. Breaks his kneecaps
And splits his shin bones.

He passes out in agony,
Eyes rolled back into his head
But a whiff of ammonia wakes him up.

When he is truly quartered,
Stumps burned and sealed,
She removes his skin,

One square inch at a time,

Pours salt on his bared flesh,
Hearing his strangled screams

Crescendo
Then ebb and fade
Like an echo,

Like his will to live
As he begs her to kill him.
She sighs and complies,

Stabbing him
In the brain
With her bloodspar.

Traitor to his country and queen.
Traitor to her love.
The king and sycophant is dead.

AFTERMATH OF WAR

Mephala lies in the palace of winds,
Basking in the wake of peace
After the end of the long and bloody war.

She wonders if her love is alive.
There has been no word from his infantry
But it is rumored that they are coming home.

He is a warrior like her,
A fighter and a survivor by nature.
He will return, she is certain of that.

The war has taught them little.
Lessons of old, rehashed again.
When will they ever learn?

Mephala closes her eyes,
Lying alone in the palace of winds,
And dreams of her love's return.

UNVICTORIOUS

Carrion sit at his window,
Curious, awaiting patiently
For death's eventual visitation.

Time has passed,
Accelerated before his eyes.
So much to do, so little time.

But he is resigned.
He's paid his dues
To the demons outside.

He unclasps his heart
And watches in the dark
As his black blood gushes forth.

Humanity's won this round,
He thinks, but in the next,
Another will emerge.

She will be faster, stronger,
Wiser than he could ever be,
Commanding the will of demons

And bending the world
Into what she believes
It should be.

Then he frowns,
As the last of his blood
Flows to the ground.

He falls facedown,
Unvictorious, he
Who failed to wear the crown.

LIFEGIVER

Margritte touches the ground
With outstretched palms,
Summoning life to sprout forth
And for spring to come.

Through the hard, crusted soil,
Saplings struggle to emerge,
But snap and break before
They can even feel the sun.

Margritte hums, asking for help.
It arrives swiftly in droves of five.
Squirrels and foxes burrow deep,
Removing rocks, loosening the soil.

Owls drop earthworms into the holes.
The earthworms dig tunnels
Where oxygen can reach, nourishing
The soil, breathing life back into it.

Raccoons and chipmunks cover
The broken ground with dried leaves
And twigs, creating a mulch,
A protective layer for undisturbed growth.

Margritte stretches out her arms
And summons the torrential rain.
The ground drinks it all in.
Come morning, the sky clears

And the first saplings emerge
From the earth, reaching toward
The sun that appears over
The brightening horizon.

In days, a forest is born.

PROMETHEUS

Prometheus watches
From the heavens,
Back into the ether
After his human skin
Fell to the worms.

His emissary
Has failed once again,
Falling foolishly
For the king who
Loved his warrior queen.

But now
The warrior
And the lifegiver
Have reunited
With the Spear.

Even Allegra
Cannot elude
Such an alchemic rebirth.
Allegra, his love.
His only love.

From the dark
Asphyxiating skies,
Prometheus smiles
At the portentous events
About to unfold.

FAIRY TALES

THE WOODS

When you enter the woods
You may find a cottage of candy
With the scent of burnt flesh
Emanating from the chimney.

Inside, there are wary children
With sharp knives, hesitant
To let you in and for good reason.
Leave them be. They will be fine.

Now walk through the vines
Into a secret alcove where
You may find a glass coffin
With a dead girl inside.

Keep jostling it.
You will dislodge a slice
Of poisoned apple in her throat
And she will come back to life.

You both won't know it now
But you have saved her from
A lifetime of servitude
And hell.

Guide her back
To the mines.
She has kinfolk there
Who are good and kind.

Afterwards,
Follow the path
To the thicket of trees
Where there are blueberries.

You may find a wolf racing by,
Chased by a girl in a red hood

Holding a crossbow,
Bloodlust in her eyes,

Her razor-sharp arrows flying
Roughshod in its wake.
Duck—
Or you'll be dead before you drop.

And then your story stops.

LITTLE RED

Little Red,
Motherless babe,
Taught to be self-sufficient
And brave at a young age.

She gathered fruit,
Hunted squirrel, trained herself
To be a sharpshooter
With the wooden crossbow she made.

Werewolves in the forest,
The local rumors howled.
Little Red was unperturbed.
She had no fear at all.

She'd fought off snakes,
Outrun grizzlies,
Shot alligators
While spearing fishes.

"But this is new," her ill Gran said,
"This is a cross between a wolf and a man.
He's wily, wicked, and dangerous too.
I worry he might outsmart you."

"Fear not, dear Gran," Little Red said.
"I'll fetch the doctor. Go back to bed.
My aim is true. If he causes trouble,
I'll take care of it."

Through the woods she walked,
Eyes ever watchful,
This fragile little girl,
Cloaked in a velvet red hood.

Predators stayed away,
Fearful of Little Red's spear.

Only the new ones in the wood
Dared to venture near.

A soft woosh betrayed his presence.
Little Red sent two shots his way.
A yowl of pain from the south.
Little Red sent four more that way.

Out leapt the werewolf,
Dripping blood like bread crumbs.
That furry crazy-eyed wolf beast,
At Little Red he lunged.

She stepped artfully aside,
Shot him another two times:
Once in the head,
Once in his eye.

Another two for posterity,
And he was down
Splayed and drunk
Like a sheep skin rug.

Little Red rushed home,
Doc in tow.
Gran was sitting up,
Unnaturally flushed.

Her smile revealed
Stalactites in the snow.
She tore the good Doc in two
Without so much as a hello.

Little Red stared in dismay.
For the first time, she could not aim.
Scarecrow-still, she watched
Gran turn, face elongating,

Arms sprouting fur, like
Seedlings in slow-motion.

Gran's nails and teeth
Grew like rabid weeds.

In her eyes,
A familiar crazed expression but
None of the love nor recognition
Little Red used to see inside.

She swung her new talons
At Little Red's head, unfroze her
With the knowledge
That this was no longer Gran.

Gran would never
Raise her hand
At her beloved granddaughter.
This was truly some other monster.

Twin head shots
Dispatched that alien thing.
Little Red wept with sadness and rage
As she carried Gran's body for burying.

Now marked
A new era for Little Red.
It was time to grow up;
Time to hunt predators instead.

GRANDMOTHER RED

One never quite recovers
From the trauma
Of being eaten.

I find myself consumed
With rage,
Still asphyxiating

Inside that wolf's
Acrid belly,
My flesh seared

By its stomach acid,
That constant sensation
Of burning

Before being cut out
And spilling into the world
Like a newborn.

This rebirth
Was not easy,
Born not of love

But of hunger,
Savagery,
And nonchalance.

I, too, transform,
Picking up her crossbow,
Hunting wolves

Till they are
But a rumor,
A whisper,

A forgotten myth.

SNOW

Cast out from home
By that jealous gnome
Her father married
When her mother passed on.

Vain and younger,
She kept an oval mirror
In her dress pocket
So it was always with her.

Constantly jealous
Of her stepdaughter's beauty
And effortless warmth
With everyone around her,

She wondered
What it was about Snow,
That inspired so many
To love and protect her.

She tested her theory
By commanding her security
To kill young Snow
And dispose of her body.

But they couldn't.
They'd known her since
She was a baby, watched her
Grow up into a gentle lady.

They snapped photos of her
Lying "slain" in red paint,
Smuggled her on a ship
In a very large crate

Taking her to an island
Far from her stepmother,

Where she was adopted by
A group of old dwarven miners

Who had recently lost
Their own wives and daughters
To a terrible outbreak of influenza
That killed almost all the villagers.

She became their den mother,
Making sure they had hot food
And fresh water, clothes laundered
And no ants in their cupboards.

They toiled in the dark mines
Where rats loved to gather
For ore they would trade to buy
Nice things for their daughter.

They were kind to her,
These fathers she'd always
Hoped for, and now she
Had seven to care for her.

Life was peaceful for Snow
And her adoptive fathers
Till visitors arrived
And one snapped her picture,

Posting it onto social media
Where her face had been tagged
Even before she was a toddler
From official pictures uploaded

By the royal photographer.
Google emailed a geotag alert
To her wicked stepmother
Who hired a hacker

To track and locate her,
Too easy these days

With location embedded
In the picture.

Proof of life confirmed,
She sent assassins after her,
Each thwarted by seven dwarves
With large iron hammers.

They would not lose
This precious new daughter.
They'd sworn an oath
To love and protect her.

So Stepmother disguised herself
As a humble villager,
And travelled in person
To find Snow and destroy her.

She had trained for some years
With a nefarious grandmaster
Who had as few qualms
As Stepmother's own mother.

She found Snow picking fruit
At the edge of the forest
And sent poison-laced flies
To land on her bananas.

Snow ate them while she cooked,
Making shrimp gravy for dinner.
It was Brag's 80th birthday
And she wanted it to be super.

As the poison worked into her,
She felt a strange numbness.
She fell backwards, eyes glazed,
Fixed on the Big Dipper.

Stepmother leapt with joy.
Snow was dead,

The thorn finally
Out of her head.

Victory dance done,
She quickly boarded
The next ferry before
The miners could pulp her.

Oh, they were heartbroken
When they finally found her,
In the mud, bananas strewn
Like petals all around her.

Dopey, the youngest,
Was a prolific healer.
He gathered some foxglove
And proceeded to feed her.

She choked and breathed,
Spewing a black poison,
Thankfully, neutralized by
Dopey's concoction.

Snow mended and lived,
Refusing reprisal.
What would that make them?
She reasoned to her fathers.

So they moved inland
Where there was no reception.
Snow believed vanishing
Was the better option.

One day, Stepmother returned,
Just to be certain.
Her mirror told her Snow lived,
Still beautiful and unburdened.

Thor and Brag were there,
Waiting for her by the harbor.

They'd been waiting there
Impatiently, every day for her.

For them, there was
No such thing as safe,
Not until the enemy
Was good and dead.

They seized her
When she arrived,
Showed her a picture of Snow,
Happy and alive,

Before smashing her head in
With their iron hammers
And gutting her
With their knives.

Snow lived out her days
In that peaceful place
With fathers who adored her,
And animals that loved her.

She never again feared
The return of her stepmother
But for the occasional nightmare
That shook and woke her

Till she sat up, drenched
In tears and horror,
Pulling out her phone
For reassurance,

Watching over and over
The video of how
Her stepmother was slain.
Only then could she sleep again.

ALWAYS A BEAST

"There's always a price to be paid
For everything a man gives you."
My mother told me when
I was old enough to listen.

But of course, I was foolish
Like most girls in love,
Never noticing the jaded faces
Of those long-suffering wives

Of the elders in the village,
Trying to muster a smile
When they heard
I was to be married.

I regaled them with stories
Of his time as a Beast and
How my love changed him
Back into a Prince.

They bowed their heads
And bit their lips,
Telling me a child
Would be my life's blessing

And truly, she is,
My beloved daughter,
Beside me here in the tower,
The same age as I was

When my mother
First warned me
Of what I know now
To be true,

For my Prince
Is once again a Beast

Despite his human face,
Snarling and slashing

With his once-clawed paws,
Throwing me across rooms
If I ever dared to be brave,
Standing up to his angry tirades,

Defending our daughter
From his scorn,
And comforting her in my arms
When he was done and gone.

I realize now there was a reason
Why he had been cursed:
To show the world
The Beast really was his true face,

For nature does not simply
Conjure beasts out of thin air.
The monster could never
Have been summoned

If he wasn't already there.
Too late for me now, trapped
And caged at the mercy
And whim of a mad king.

No long thick braid
Or a dragon to escape,
But an endless fall
Down the tower.

But perhaps… wait.
One day,
We might be able
To flee this place.

My daughter's hair
Has now reached her waist.

RAPUNZEL

Rapunzel did not want
To let down her hair anymore.
She was done with all that.

She tied her braid
To the iron ring
Attached to the tower wall,

And with a mirror shard,
Swiftly sawed off her hair
She'd kept since she was little.

By morning,
She'd carefully
Climbed down the tower

Using her braid as a rope,
Her pale smiling face basked
In the sunlight,

Feeling the joy of freedom
And endless possibilities,
Euphoric and hopeful,

As she vanished
Into the city
Where she'd never be recognized.

Six weeks later,
While working as a barista
To save money and flee further,

She saw a news report
Of the old queen trapped
In an abandoned tower

South of her castle
That no one realized
Was there

Until a group of schoolchildren
On vacation, stumbled upon it
While adventuring.

The army sent an extraction team
In a helicopter,
Only getting her out

After smashing
The topmost window of the tower,
Where forensics found,

In horror,
The chains on the walls,
And the paintings

That told the tale
Of a child growing up
Locked up,

A child rumored
To be the baby girl
She never wanted.

The queen was questioned
And grilled,
But never found guilty.

By that time, Rapunzel
Had crossed the border
With her hard-earned savings

To a neutral country
Where she could vanish
Into the crowd,

Finally living the life
She had always
Dreamed about.

THE GIRL FROM THE TOWER

Long have I wondered
What it is like to be free,
Racing through a forest,
Lying down by a river
Listening to an old frog sing.

I see the vast, beautiful world
From the domed-stone arch
Of a tall tower window,
My home for as long
As I can remember.

How I long to wander
Freely through the forest,
Barefoot on soft emerald grass,
Not this hard cold floor
Turning my bones to frost.

I have lived here
Since the day I was born
With my mother
Who died in my arms
During the coldest winter.

That day,
She made me promise
I'd find a way out of this tower
And to never make the mistake
Of marrying a man with power.

When my father left her for another,
He locked us up in this tower,
Telling the world we were dead
Before marrying that other woman
And having another three children.

My mother wept for a while

Before gathering herself together,
Teaching me all I needed to know
About surviving in the world outside.
One day we would flee, she assured me.

But she did not live to see this.
She died peacefully in my arms
With a smile on her face.
She was free at last, and she knew
I would fulfil her promise.

So I grow my hair long,
Carve knives out of firewood,
Run sprints in the space I have,
And build up my strength
With pushups and the plank.

The day arrives when the fog rolls in.
I drop my heavy braid
Out of the window.
It hangs taut all the way down
To the grass patch below.

I gather my things in a bag:
A painting of my mother,
The stuffed cat she made me
When I was just a baby,
And my collection of carved knives.

Around the cast-iron ring,
Once used to torture prisoners,
I tie my hair into a dead knot
Before sawing it off, yanking it hard
To ensure it can take my entire weight.

Then I climb, one step at a time,
As the north wind threatens
To blow me down,
But I hold on,
Reaching the ground,

Not stopping a moment
To look back,
I race into the woods,
Barefoot on the soft mossy grass,
Reaching the river bank

Where I lay myself down,
Listening to an old frog sing.
Now I rest. Now I mourn.
Tomorrow I will plan
How to take my father down.

GIRL ON FIRE

For Minz and Maunz who had to see this

Little girl
Plays with matches
While her parents are out.

The cats wail for her to stop.

Too late!
The flames light her up
Like a Christmas tree.

Her poor cats cry out for help.

She burns and burns
Till she is ash
And bone.

The cats weep a brook in their home.

(Reinterpreted from Heinrich Hoffmann's *Die gar traurige Geschichte mit dem Feuerzeug in Struwwelpeter*)

JACK AND THE GIANTS

In the oldest part
Of Dragonbeard town,
There lived a boy, Jack,
And his sickly old mom.

When their money ran out,
Jack would not sell the cow.
Bessie gave them milk.
She did not deserve the cull.

Jack took a job carrying
Heavy bags of wheat.
He was bone tired,
Working week after week.

Still, he helped an old woman
With her large hefty cart.
He dragged it all the way up
The rocky mountaintop.

Grateful for his kindness,
She gave him a bag of seeds,
Told him to plant them
Where the sun never sleeps.

In a day, they sprouted,
Each one different.
One produced potatoes,
Another one, carrots.

Yet another grew lettuce
And the tastiest apples.
The tallest one produced no fruit.
It grew and grew way past the roof.

In time, it grew beyond
The tallest cloud,

Its base deeply rooted,
Standing strong and proud.

Jack had a dream:
He climbed to the top
And found something
He thought he had lost.

In the morning, he grasped
The strong wiry branches,
Climbed up and up, through
The fat, fluffy clouds, and found

An island floating in the sky
Covered with emerald grass,
An azure pond,
A huge cottage fit for a god.

The doorway stood like a gate to hell,
Windows built like gargantuan cells.
Through the grilles he slipped
Into the enormous house

And heard a thunderous voice
Booming strong and loud,
"Fee fi fo fum, I smell
The flesh of a human rump."

"No, no!"
Screamed a familiar voice.
Could it be the father
He thought was gone?

Jack drew his dagger,
Encased in bull leather.
A shiny old thing
From his stolid grandmother.

In the kitchen, he found
People locked in tall cages,

Dangling above a Giant
Seated before a furnace.

There on the table, his father,
Tied down on a grilling plate,
Buttered and basted
And ready to be baked!

Jack thought fast.
He shoved a slab of butter
Just below the oven door,
Climbed to the highest point,

Where he leapt
Onto the Giant's shoulder,
Sticking his dagger
Into the back of his neck.

But it barely broke his flesh,
And in the Giant's anger,
He took two steps forward
And slipped on the butter,

The momentum pushing him
Into the burning fire.
Jack jumped off in time,
Grasping the furnace handle,

The Giant's forward force
Slamming the door shut.
The people cheered and pointed
To a lever that would free them.

He nodded,
Untied his father first,
Embracing the old man
He hadn't seen in years.

Together, they freed
The remaining strangers,

Each climbing down carefully
Till they reached the earth.

Jack's family was reunited,
And he, hailed a hero,
His family revered
By the grateful people.

The old woman
Who gave him the seeds
Embraced her lost sons,
Her mission done.

The news spread far and wide
And people now queried
If their lost ones, too,
Were imprisoned in the clouds.

Jack grew up,
Became a great warrior.
In the war against the Giants,
He led the charge.

HANSEL AND GRETEL

Hansel and Gretel lived with
Their father and stepmother
After their loving mom
Suddenly died of cancer.

Their father's new wife told him
To get rid of the children.
She said she'd love him better
If they were no longer with him.

So he took them for a walk
Into the deep, dark forest,
And left them there
To a wintry death sentence.

"I'll return soon," he promised,
Before leaving like a coward.
Gretel had a bad feeling, but
Thought, *he'd never abandon us.*

By nightfall, she was less certain
As the winter cold set in.
The children started walking
On a path they'd never been.

They spied a candy cottage
Surrounded with tall trees.
On the porch was an old woman
Who beckoned them in.

"You must be freezing from
The blistering cold breeze."
The children, out of options,
Embraced her hospitality.

For days they stayed,
Enjoying her splendid cooking.

The stewed meat tasted strange
But the children chose to ignore it.

One day, she asked Hansel
To help her check the oven.
Some fuse had apparently burst
And now it was broken.

Hansel bent down to crawl in
As the old woman hovered,
Arms outstretched,
As if to push him in it.

Gretel acted fast, and with
A running start, shoved
The old woman into the oven
Just as Hansel stood up.

Gretel suspected foul play
Right from the start—
The countless figurines
Carved out of bone. Odd,

Since there was no game
Left in the forest.
But the meat:
Where did it come from?

Gretel tried hard
Not to think about that one.
The snow still blew strong,
But the children had time.

There was no way to open
The oven from inside.
They found remains
In the kitchen larder.

Small skeletons, like theirs.
Those children,
Missing for years.
One of them, a friend of hers.

"It has to be done,"
Gretel told her brother.
"Think of all the children
She could potentially slaughter."

The old woman confessed
After three days inside.
The children shook their heads
And left her to die.

They turned on the oven,
Ignoring her screams
And pounding fists
As she burned alive.

When she was ash and bone,
They cleaned out the oven,
Then burned the remains
Of the other children.

There, they stayed
Until winter was over,
Surviving on candy
And four-leaved clovers.

Soon, spring arrived
With the first curious deer
And shortly after,
A wolf that wandered near.

Hansel and Gretel thought hard
About their future—
About those who failed them
And the terrible world outside.

It was easy to decide.
They chose to stay
And made the cottage their own.
In time, it would feel just like home.

THE MERMAID

Once I dreamed
Of my days of youth
When I walked
On shores with sand.

I fell in love
With a haunting song
And the face
That came along.

How we loved
Like siren gods
Till he killed me
With a nod.

His men threw me back
Into the guileless sea,
Limbless
And reborn.

She took my voice
And she took my soul
As I traded them
For revenge.

The scythe I swung
Curved beautifully,
Leaving arcs
Of the crescent moon.

I gave his head
To the old sea witch
Who happily
Completed the spell.

Now I walk
With human skin

And two strong legs,
Free as the wind.

I miss my tail
But not as much
As the forgotten depths
Of my human soul.

BEAUTY SLEEPS FOR A CENTURY

Born into royalty,
The first female child in a century,
Her parents named her Beauty,
For her porcelain white skin
And her sweet angelic face.

12 good fairies attended
Her christening, bestowing
Gifts of kindness and artistry,
Intelligence and generosity,
Traits a princess should have.

The uninvited 13th fairy,
Banished for always bringing
Chaos and cruelty,
Crashed the party
And cursed the poor baby:

She'll be pricked
By a spindle's needle
And be dead before 30.
With that, she cackled
At her triumphant victory,

And left with a fruit cake,
Humming a ditty, something
About sewing and diddly,
Vanishing through the grand exit
Before anyone could say a word.

The 12th fairy, who was still
Thinking of a gift, decided
To try and reverse the spell,
Saving poor Beauty from
A life of fear and misery.

The laws of magic allowed her

To amend it to a century's sleep
Instead of a permanent death—
A much more preferable gift.
But also to add a twist,

Because the 12th fairy,
Second youngest in the family,
Was a romantic at heart,
She stipulated that Beauty
Had to be kissed

By a handsome prince
Before the spell could lift.
The Queen wept in despair
At the illogical whims of the fairies
And their unfathomable spells!

The King decreed for all spindles
To be smashed into kindling,
Except for the metal parts,
Which were to be remade into swords.
He was a great advocate of recycling.

Beauty at 15 was a curious child,
Vanishing for hours, alarming them all.
She discovered secret alcoves and rooms,
Even hidden passages to the kitchen
For those who loved food.

The 10th fairy's gift—curiosity—
Proved to be Beauty's undoing.
Knowing quite well
Of the young girl's wanderings,
The 13th fairy removed

Her cloaking spell,
Unveiling a secret room
She'd previously installed.
A spindle sat smack in the middle,
And wearing an old woman's skin,

She invited Beauty in,
Showing the curious girl
How to work the spindle,
And invariably, Beauty
Got poked by the needle,

Free falling into darkness,
Taunted by the resounding echo
Of the 13th fairy's maniacal laughter
While everyone in the castle
Suddenly fell fast asleep

And a thorny thicket wound tight
Around the castle,
As if to protect it,
Until a hundred years later,
When a courageous Prince

From a faraway land,
Heard of the tragic story
And resolved to save
Everyone in it.
Travelling across the world,

It took months after he set sail
Before he finally arrived
At the castle gates.
He cut through the thicket
Of wild branches alone.

Thorns ripped through his armor,
Tearing into his bones.
Ignoring the pain, he forged on,
Reaching the castle doors,
Pushing them open,

Searching room by room
As blood poured profusely
From his wounds,

Leaving
A long crimson trail.

He finally found her asleep
Inside that secret chamber,
Knelt beside her like a groom,
Empathy filling his heart
Despite all of his blood loss.

He knew what he needed to do
To break the terrible spell.
The 12th fairy
Whom he tracked down
Had advised him well.

With what strength he had left,
He gently bent over Beauty
And kissed her softly on the lips
Then fell across her,
Breathing his last.

Beauty woke up,
Shoved the stranger off her body,
Grabbed the spindle's needle
And stabbed the old woman dead
Before the 13th fairy woke up

And registered her folly
Of remaining in human skin
After her triumphant spell,
Which really, did not go well
Since her sister altered the spell.

Beauty stood and stretched.
It had been a hundred years
Of mad dreams and cruel fairies.
Now it was time to kill them all
And reclaim her land and her story.

CINDERELLA

The rocks spoke to me
That night at the ball,
The one where I was meant
To end it all.

Dancing with the Prince
Brought me to this place,
By the cliff wall where
The ancient rocks prayed,

Telling me
There must be another way.
Killing the Prince
Would not change my fate.

The monsters were at home,
Not in the castle where
I'd long imagined
There lived a dozen trolls

Conjuring magic
To keep me at my post.
That's what my father told
A very little girl.

The rocks showed me
A flashback of my life:
Thrown into the cinders
The moment my mother died.

How quickly Father took in
Stepmother and her spawn.
It showed me my worth,
Telling me never again to fawn.

I was back in the Prince's arms.
His eyes were kind,

Unlike Father's, full of scorn,
As if he hated that I was born.

I pressed my dagger
Back into its sheath,
Smiled at the Prince
And danced all night long.

At dawn,
The carriage took me home
Where I scrubbed myself
Clean to the bone.

That evening, the Prince
Found me alone at home,
Dressed in my ball gown
With a peaceful smile.

I found my true happiness
As queen, at last,
While the true monsters
Lie buried, deep underground.

LIVING WELL IS THE BEST REVENGE

I am my mother's child.
Those who remember her
Always tell me this, despite
Not remembering her very well.

The things I did—poisoning
My stepsisters with arsenic
And placing ground-up glass
In their slippers—were justice.

Nothing prepares a child
To be treated the way I was,
Cast into the cinders and told
I shouldn't have been born,

Justifying everything they did
With their fists and their feet
Till I was eight then they switched
To sheer contempt and words of hate.

But now I am queen
And they have shorter toes
And ugly skin, a more suitable
Punishment, I tell myself.

Often, I think about flaying
My father and stepmother,
Slowly beheading my stepsisters,
Pulling their guts out with my fingers.

Some things cannot be forgotten.
Or forgiven.

So after supper, when all
The good folk are asleep,
I will bring my wolf and my bike,
My cloak and my knife

Out for a long and bloody night.

NEVER HAPPY AFTER

It'd be so poetic to stab them
With my old glass slippers,
But that would leave far
Too much evidence behind.

Instead, I bide my time,
Wait till the stars align,
Find my way back to the castle,
Where you've made a home with her,

The courtier, infamous
For destroying families.
For fun, for sport, no one knows,
But everyone condemns her terrible deeds—

Mere whispers in the castle till today
When I slice her in two, head to groin,
Both halves falling onto the throne room floor,
Creating a path for me and my scythe

To reach him, cowering in a corner,
Begging for his life,
Which does not move me
But fuels my rage at the waste,

At a decade's worth of indignities
And his dark, callous cruelty.
I do not hesitate,
Slashing him into pieces,

My scythe making graceful strokes,
Imitating the masters, splattering
His blood all over the marble wall.
It is still an art piece I marvel at today,

Walking to the throne, scythe returned
To its rightful owner who was glad

To take a break and lend me the reins.
"Well done," Death says,

Patting my arm as I put on the crown,
A faint glimpse of pride beams in her face.
From that day forth, my dreams are sweet,
Covered in blood and sleet.

And oh, do I welcome it.

ALL THE MONSTERS IN THE WORLD

WHEN THERE ARE MONSTERS

When there are monsters in the house,
You learn to move silently in the dark,
Tread lightly on tiptoe, make no sound.

You learn to lock doors behind you,
Slowly and softly so they won't
Follow you in and surprise you,

Corner you and maim you,
Invade you and desecrate you,
Then discard you when they are done

With what's left of you,
In bloody shards, broken and burnt,
Most of you lost in ashes.

You awake the next day,
Raw, in pain,
Gingerly

Walking and talking
Like a person,
But there is nothing there. Not anymore.

When there's a monster in the house,
You learn to duck behind doors
And walk with the shadows.

The dark is far safer than the light
Where monsters can see you,
Seize you and destroy you

When you let your guard down
And forget just for a moment—
They always move faster than you.

So I have joined the darkness.
I have joined the shadows.
No one can touch me in the dark.

THE MONSTERS WITHIN

You follow me everywhere

Unburdened by sealed doors
And encased windows,
Always too close
For me to escape you.

For a time, I thought
You were my shadow,
A will-o'-the-wisp,
A ghost,

But these bloodied bodies
I wake up beside tell me
That like me,
You are corporeal.

I hoped you would help me
Clean up your kills,
But you never appear
When you are needed.

Instead, I've become
An expert in body disposal,
For no one would believe
I did not do what you did.

Today, I see you
Wearing my face
In the mirror.
I know the truth.

Mother told me the secret
In a reluctant phone call,
How we fought to the death
In her womb

While she watched,
Horrified,
Through the ultrasound.
Afterwards, I ate you.

For far too long,
I have lived in your shadow.
But now, dear twin,
We are truly one.

I no longer fear you.

MEMOIRS IN THE DARK

The bones graze my throat
As they go down, scraping
Away the infection.

But too late.
It has seeped into my core,
Changing me permanently.

We fade into the shadows,
Moving into the basement.
The faint glimmer of sun rays,

Our only source of light,
Illuminating the moss gardens
That keep us company and sane

While the cat slips out at night
To patrol and pick fights
With the next door cat.

Sometimes she brings
A bird or a rat.
On that night, we feast

And sleep like cherubs,
Curled up in our wings,
Dreaming of a world

Of darkness and peace,
Without the death touch
Of humanity.

Soon, the only sounds
Are the songs of crickets
And the gentle rumbling

Of thunder

And distant screams
Till the silence drowns out

Everything.
As it does,
Inevitably,

The world falls into chaos
When the apocalypse descends.
I decide then it is time

To rejoin it.

DARK DRAGONS

Wild sea breeze on our skins,
We carve your name in sand

Remembering you fondly
While sipping milkshakes

On the beach where
We misspent our youth

Dreaming about motorcycles
And beautiful girls.

Your voice like a boombox,
Your love for Vivaldi.

Your three angels
Always orbiting you

Like planets
Around their dazzling star.

Your brilliant career,
Setting you up for life.

The house on the hill,
The fast cars, all yours at 22.

Your love for good brandy
And fine company.

How you died—
Forever a mystery.

We burn what remains of you
On the sun-scorched sand.

The clouds shift,
Forming dark dragons.

VIOLATION

My only crime is my youth.
Are you jealous
Or just covetous?
My body is mine,
From infancy till adulthood.
That's the way
It's supposed to be.

But now as I touch
The remaining shards
Of my girlhood,
I rage
As you drag me
Screaming
Through the woods.

My head hits a stone,
Cracking my skull.
I bounce over a rock
Severing my spine,
Breaking my bones.
The law will not help.
It is made up of you.

You gouge out my eyes
So I cannot see you
Tearing off my flesh,
Claiming it for your own.
In my mind's eye
I see only Momma,
My only-ever anchor.

Momma! I am losing
Ownership of my body.
My identity, barely formed,
Is stripped away from me.
I call to my sister to *Run! Run!*

There is no more hope for me.
But there is hope for her.

I am six.
She is only three.

THE HAUNTING

There's a rattling
And a dull clank
From the ceiling again.

I wonder
If the murdered child
Is still haunting its parents.

Just yesterday,
I saw the mother,
Dark and hollow-eyed,

Tears matted all over her face,
And the father,
Pale as a ghost

And half his weight,
Both of them shuffling
Like shadows down the stairs

With a small black cloud
Tagging along
Just a few paces behind.

It'll be another sleepless night
For the three of us—an irony—
When only one of us is the murderer,

And only one without care or conscience.

THE NECROMANCY PROGRAM

Necromancy 101~
 The tombstones
 Stir and shift

Necromancy 201~
 Scratching
 In the graves

Necromancy 301~
 First rising
 From the dead

Necromancy 401~
 The cemetery
 Empty at dawn

CONCEPTS

Monsters are not real,
I tell my son constantly
Despite his older cousin
Saying otherwise.

The devil is a concept,
Something someone made up
A long time ago, to frighten
Others into submission.

Don't say devil, he cries.
It is a concept, I gently
Remind him, just like unicorns
And drakes, phoenixes and dragons,

The tooth fairy, even old Santa,
Whom you know now is not real,
All wonderful concepts we made up
To make life more interesting.

I tuck him in, safe and tight,
Stroke and kiss his chilly skin.
He looks at me with wide eyes,
Momma, are humans real?

I laugh. Of course, my son.
They are our food, our lifeline.
When you are 12, I will teach you
How to hunt and how to feed.

Till then, only sweet dreams
Of warm blood and the moon.
I kiss his forehead
And gently close the coffin.

NEVER THE LIGHT

There was something
About the light
That always hurt my eyes.

I never knew what it was
Till my fangs first emerged
And sheared off half my lips.

When was I turned?
How could I not know?
It was a mystery

Till I called my mother
Who confessed
It was in our blood,

A gift when we reached
The age of adulthood,
A defence in this world for us.

I wept in gratitude,
Looking at the body,
Desiccated before me,

The man who supposedly
Loved me but hit me, repeatedly,
Now curled dead at my feet.

Be strong, be brave,
My mother said in dulcet tones.
No one will ever hurt you again.

THE ISLAND

So there they are,
The twin boats
That brought us
To this end,

Perched by the shore
To forever watch
The beatific sun rise
And fall with the tides

While our bodies
Decompose in solitude
By the wilting coconut trees
Surely resentful of our presence

But grateful when we finally
Break down and give them
A rush of nutrients to flower
Some fat coconuts for the monkeys.

Perhaps only then am I
Willing to leave, knowing
My life will be of some use
To the universe.

I do not move
My broken shattered body
But turn my eyes
To the stars

Enjoying a moment
Of quiet serenity
Before the wretched
Monkeys take them.

INTO THE TALL GRASS

Vermillion plumes rise
From the black towers.
Who are they burning today?

I clutch the children tight,
Relieved we ran when we did,
Safe for now in the wilderness.

In the tower pyres,
The Overlords are culling again,
Our elders rounded up

And incinerated
To fuel the engines and run the city,
And to make room for the young.

Father grasps my hand,
Thinking of his friends left behind,
All of them on the culling list.

Are they in the plumes tonight?
Or are they still safe and alive
In their concrete homes?

We will never know.
It is time to move.
We have stayed here too long.

Soon,
Someone will notice
We are missing

And the Overlords
Will send Hunters after us.
They are merciless.

Wasp-sized, their bites paralyze

And inject a tracker
For the retrieval team to collect us.

After all,
We are fuel for the furnace,
An energy source for the city.

Someone needs to feed the monster.
And the Overlords think,
Better them than us.

I beg everyone to walk a little faster
But they tire.
We rest.

Minutes later,
A familiar buzzing fills the air.
The Hunters have found us.

Father tells me
To take the children and go.
He will distract the Hunters

To allow us to escape, undetected.
"The children need their mother,"
He whispers, urgently.

I shake my head
And pull him back.
"They also need their grandfather!"

The Hunters are almost upon us.
Before us, a river looms.
We run.

"Get into the water!" Father cries.
We lie face up in the shallows,
Eyes closed, staying calm.

We have practiced this

For a long time.
And after a song,

Ten songs,
They pass us by
And go home.

Only now
Will they conclude
We have died.

I should know.
They were my design—
The Hunters I created

Were for our defence
Against the aliens,
Not our own people.

I protested.
So they sentenced me to die,
Along with everyone I love.

Not all of us made it out.
We saw the rest caught
And executed on the spot,

Even our family dog
Who fought bravely
To take them down.

I hold Father and my children tight.
For the first time since we fled,
I let myself cry.

Freedom has never tasted sweeter.
Life, never more precious.
Finally, we are free from the Overlords.

We fill our bottles with water

And head south, along the river.
We will cross the forest

Into the desert,
Through the sand dunes
To an oasis where it is safe.

I tell them this
To give them hope.
But there is nothing out here.

Nothing I know of.
Only death.
But hopefully,

A death
That will be far away from now.
Somehow, we will live.

Somehow, we will thrive.
We take our first step
Into the tall grass.

THE GIRL MADE OF ELECTRICITY

The girl made of electricity
Avoided all water, hid indoors
When it rained, covered herself
With a shock-proof silicone suit.

She avoided human contact
As any touch released a deathly charge.
That was how she lost
Everyone she loved.

But when the rain did not stop
And the flood waters rose,
And the endless storms drowned
Everything they touched,

The girl made of electricity
Decided she was done with the world,
This game that cost her everything,
Everything that gave her life meaning.

She removed her suit, crackling
With power, stood on the roof
As lightning struck her once, twice,
Three times until she was pure energy.

Into the waters she leapt,
Electrocuting everything
Till the flood receded
And the ground was calm.

All the rescue teams found
Were the silver-white bones
Of the dead and a skeleton
Made of diamond stone.

And then it rose.

THE LADY OF THE LAKE

Under the smile of the full moon,
She skates silently, graceful as a swan,
Drawing figure eights onto the frozen lake.

Four men leap out of the brush,
Knives brandished, teeth bared,
Reaching for the skater with fiendish intent.

Their combined weight tears open the ground
And they fall through, flailing like drowning rats
In the cold frigid ice.

The Lady of the Lake pirouettes and sings,
Summoning her children to rise from the depths.
It is feeding time.

REFLECTIONS

Do not take
A moment to rest,
For all you have done
Will flood you with emotion.

Instead, keep busy
And do not reflect on
Your blood-soaked hands,
Your cherry-stained mouth,

For it is no crime
To drink and celebrate
These long millennia
We've had together.

ALL THE MONSTERS IN THE WORLD

Two minutes remaining.
We dash out of the clearing
And there, the abandoned boat
Lying sideways on the shore,

Too heavy for us to push
But we try anyway,
Channelling what remains
Of our dwindling adrenaline stores.

The sound of thundering footsteps
And furious ravenous screams
Spur us on to push and push
Till we see an inch of give

And then a foot and then another
Till gravity helps us out
By sliding the old boat
Swiftly into the water

Just as the monsters emerge,
Shrieking and shaking with rage,
Their prey just out of reach.
Now they turn on each other.

I hold my children close
Till the island's out of sight.
We remember those we lost,
No longer the people we love,

Ghouls on a desert island,
No longer our island home.
"Where do we go now, Mom?"
My littlest daughter asks.

"We will find a place, somehow,
Somewhere safe, I promise.

Far from this plague I created
To reset our dying world."

The expanse of sea surrounds us.
Death surrounds us.
A world of possibilities surrounds us.
Hope surrounds us.

THE CAPACITY OF VIOLENCE

THE JOY OF SEWING

Tired of her speaking,
He sewed her lips shut,
Never imagining she would
Take so well to the needle
And thread that she began
Her own darning of him
As he slept, sewing finger
To finger and leg to leg
And toe to toe and head
To shoulder so that when
He awoke he could still
See and scream for she
Spared his eyes and mouth
For the joy of his grief.

MORTAL LIFE

It's been barely an hour
Since you left me for dead,
Snoring drunk beside me
After you took off my head.

I clamber out blindly,
Out of the bloody bed,
Searching high and low
For needle and thread.

But first, the duct tape
To fasten my head,
Align it nicely
So I won't make a mistake.

It takes a gallon of superglue,
But I am back from the dead,
Ravenous and enraged,
And out for your head.

I take the sharpest knife,
The one Grandma gave me
When I was a young bride,
When I was stupid and nice.

Your rhythmic breathing
Tells me you're still alive
But not when I slice and dice
And gouge out your eyes.

You've always told me
That I warm up your heart.
I throw it in the fire,
Now, that's a start.

LOBOTOMY

She wakes up, her head in a fog.
There is a vast chasm in her chest cavity,
As if someone snuck into her room at night
And removed her heart.

It is just as well, she thinks.
Emotions are destructive to one's sanity,
And hers have long been lost
To the perils of ill-fated love,

Displaced anger,
And immeasurable sadness
Over things that cannot be done,
And things that cannot be undone.

She sighs, expelling the exhausted breath
From her beaten lungs into the stale cold air
That surrounds and embraces her.
In that moment, a revelation dawns.

The instrument weighs strangely light in her hand.
She knows what to do.
She's seen it performed a million times before
As the good doctor's assistant.

A sharp thrust up
Through the inner corner of her eye
And then out. It is done.
If she could feel joy, she would have smiled.

INHERITANCE

She drove up the long driveway
As the dead followed her
Through the old, familiar grounds
Where she once played as a child.
Haunted, whispered the locals.
But she did not believe in such lies.

Turn back, turn back,
Or die like the rest.

The voices sang in her head
As she turned the corner, arriving
At the massive mansion, now moldy
And grimy with age and disrepair.
She parked the car and walked up
The massive steps meant for giants.

Go away, go away,
We do not want to play.

She stabbed the key into the lock.
It protested with a creak
But she shoved it open anyway.
The lights were out
But she was unperturbed.
She was no longer afraid of the dark.

Tick, tock, we will
Pluck your heart out.

She returned to the car
To fetch her portable torch.
It lit up a shroud of dust
In the hollow, empty hall.
Then, she heard a door slam,
Echoing like a concussion.

Come, come,
Come to the basement.

Yes, where the bad things happened.
The door was ajar. A haloed light
Around it shone like false hope.
She shoved the door open with her foot.
Each step creaked as she walked down.
And there it was, shiny and blue.

Machines to scare people,
Keep them away. So I can play.

She remembered this place.
And she remembered him.
The sweets and the toys,
All to lure her here. For terror.
And his sick pleasure. There,
He sat now, his back to her.

Old baseball bat. You won me
Trophies. Now do me a solid.

She swung hard and it connected
With his skull, over and over
Until his head was gone.
She left the house in flames.
He would hurt no child again.
Soon, she received the insurance cheque.

Rebuild, rebuild,
And start over again.

REPARATION

Yesterday you walked
In your skin and your bones
As you breathed out poison,
Destroying families and homes.

You care nothing
For the deaths in your wake,
But for the lives you'd steal
And the furs that you'd take.

See my scythe,
Keep it in your eye.
Now see your body
Lying in the sty.

We have moved
To the sacred place in the sky,
Watching you weep,
Watching you die.

THE FOREST OF DISCARDED BABY GIRLS

No man dares enter
The forest of discarded baby girls
After sundown in the dead of night.

The wind howls
When another girl is abandoned,
Always at the edge of the forest

By her complicit father
And weeping mother,
Held at knifepoint by the elders.

Any mother who refuses
Is stabbed repeatedly
Till she falls,

Heart hollow, eyes dead,
Her final thought:
Despair

At failing her baby,
While her husband flees
From the forest,

Their daughter
Slowly fed
To the ground.

The trees sway and weep
As the baby screams all night
Until day finally breaks

And her cry is cut short.
The forest has embraced her
As one of its own.

When they are grown,

The daughters return home,
Each strangling the man

Who discarded her at birth
With winding branches
That emerge from her fingers.

Afterwards,
She burns his house down
And gathers her mother

Back to the forest,
The only true place
They can call home.

ANNALISE WANDERS THE FOREST

Annalise wanders the forest

Free from those
Who tried to hang her
For seeking justice in a world
Where it does not exist.

She tore off her noose,
Enraged at the executioner
Who cowered in terror—
He saw her neck break

When he kicked the stool out
From under her,
Watched her struggle and kick
Until she was still

But for a minute
Before her eyes opened again,
Wide, darting, remembering,
Then training onto him.

In a swift movement
Too fast for everyone's eyes,
She ripped his head clean off
And flung it into the crowd.

Screams filled her ears,
A sweet operetta she remembered
Her father bringing her to watch
When she was just a child.

It was the same crowd,
Watching her execution,
Scattering in terror now
As she picked up an axe

From the ground.
They should not have come
To cheer on her death
But they did.

Executions were one of
Their few entertainments.
But death should be mourned,
Not celebrated, Annalise thought.

Yet the joy she felt slashing
Each observer to bloody shreds
Brought a peace and a catharsis
From the justice it served.

)

Annalise wanders the forest

Free at last
But then she sees a young fawn,
Dead on the ground, arrows
Protruding from its stomach.

She turns
And walks back into the world,
Back to civilization,
Where there is still

Much justice to be served.

THE DEER

Even the weeds
Taste bitter and wrong.

The deer knows
Their food is now poisoned.

Those metal birds
Have been flying over her forest,

Releasing a toxic rain that falls
Far too much and far too often.

Furless apes
That wear the skins of others

Are spraying mist
All over the foliage.

She finds one collapsed,
Leg twisted under itself.

Starving,
She bites it in anger.

Its flesh is unexpectedly
Sweet and delicious.

Energized, she takes another bite.
And another.

NOONWRAITHS

On the hottest day of summer,
The noonwraiths gather
In the cornfields,

Beneath the scorching sun,
Dried garlands still
In their matted hair,

Dressed in their wedding gowns,
The same ones they wore
When they died,

Refusing to give in
To the darkest traditions of men,
The same ones that broke

And enslaved them,
Turning them
Into mere vessels and wombs,

Not equals with feelings,
With rights,
With hearts and minds.

I feel an ache in my neck
Whenever they are near,
Each scorching summer

When they return for
The worst of their betrothed
Amid the tall stalks of corn.

I have seen them,
Surrounding him
While he works,

Placing their hands on him,

Burning him alive,
Cooking him from the inside.

The people call it heatstroke,
Refusing to believe in ghosts.
But I know otherwise.

The year I turn 13,
My father sells me
To the farmer next door:

The one with the reputation,
The one who beat
His young wives to death

And bought off the town
And bought off the sheriff.
The one who is untouchable.

But the acres of land
Papa will receive
In exchange for me

Is worth much more
To the family than
Another mouth to feed.

The trade is made.
And each night I weep
And pray for God to save me.

But He does nothing,
Leaving me, prepubescent me
In a clean white dress,

Waiting for my father
To give me away—
Livestock to the slaughter.

So I call to the noonwraiths.

I call them by their names.
I remember each of them

From the countless Saturdays
I brought corn to their doors
For a fair exchange.

And like true sisters,
They come to my aid,
Sweeping through the county,

Immolating the monsters
With their touch,
With blue fire.

I race out of my room
To watch the wedding barn burn,
Papa and my betrothed

Both dancing in flames,
Arms outstretched
As if they can fly

But instead,
They lose their wings
And fall dead onto the ground.

Then as if they were never here,
The noonwraiths dissipate
Into the wind

And I inhale,
Breathing them in,
Soaking in the scorched air,

The intoxicating scent of freedom.
Now they are in me,
And I, in them.

FOREST MOTHER

I return to the roots,
The branches, the leaves,
To the only place
I ever found peace.

In this palace of winds
I am one with the trees,
The crows and the ravens
Bring solace to me.

No devastation from men
With their sticks and knives,
No destruction from those
Labelling me with a price.

Here I am now
With the sticks and stones,
Here I will reduce
Them all into bones.

They will arrive
With their guns and scythes,
Here we will wait
And eat them alive.

THE SACRIFICE

She lays herself onto the ground.
On her pale young face, a painful frown.

She blinks away her gathering tears,
Reminding herself of the things at stake—

Her parents held with guns to their heads
To be shot point blank if the trade isn't made.

So she waits, the chosen one, brave but afraid
Till the monster looms, tall and great.

He picks her up with his giant claw,
Pops her in his mouth, ready to eat her raw.

Before he bites down, she pulls out a gun,
Shoots him right through his thick bony skull.

He falls down heavily onto the ground.
She crawls out, looking cautiously around.

The townsfolk have fled, her parents
Dead, gun shots to their heads.

She screams out loud in a primal rage.
The resonance shatters all of their bones.

She sets fire to that hateful world.
The old cottages burn, slowly unfurl.

She walks away, down an unknown road
In search for a new place she can call home.

ONE DARK NIGHT

Our bags are packed,
Waiting like sentinels
By the front door

Where the twins stand,
Hand-in-hand, half-asleep,
Half a foot in dreams.

He has passed out
Drunk yet again
With bloody fists.

I've long given up
On him ever changing,
My face battered

Black and blue
Enough times
To never forget it.

I can only start anew
With my crone powers
Slowly awakening.

My fingertips tingle
With a lightning crackle.
I touch the door,

Watching it blaze
With azure fire
As it tears open a portal

Into an emerald-green world,
Full of cotton candy clouds
And crystal clear ponds

Floating beside them

On languid leafy pads,
Magic carpets in the air.

The twins do not hesitate.
Their eyes light up
And each picks up a suitcase.

"Let's go, Momma,"
They plead with eager eyes.
"It must be better

On the other side."
I nod,
Clasping their hands.

We take a deep breath
And step into the portal.
It is as magical as I imagined.

I turn back to close
The barrier between
Our worlds forever

But first, I send through
A sprinkling of silver stardust,
Imploding the house

As the portal seals shut.

THE DOLLS

The paralytic works perfectly.

Eyes wide and frozen,
She succumbs to the spell,

Pickling her insides,
Drying her skin

Which I polish
Till it gleams,

Plastic Barbie face,
Raggedy Ann hair

I hand-weave from
The cords of cotton

I used
To strangle her with.

Her eyes bulged
As she passed out,

Making it easy
To pop them out.

In her eye sockets,
I insert the buttons

From her coat.
With a good shove

And a swab of hot glue,
They stay put,

One in each groove.
Yes, she can feel that too.

I tie her by her hair
To the clothesline

Across the laundry room
Where I can sit and watch

The lovely row
Of dangling dolls

Who were once
My husband's mistresses.

Tomorrow,
He will join them too.

THE TOOTH COLLECTOR

Some people collect stamps.
I collect teeth,
Mostly from terrible people.

You see,
I was born
With a capacity for violence

And in the world
I grew up in,
It was necessary.

I haunt the streets
Where monsters hide
In plain sight,

Waiting to seize
Young girls
In broad daylight.

Here's where I step in.
I grab his hand
Holding the girl,

Snapping back his fingers,
Breaking his hold.
I tell her to run

While I twist and pull,
Breaking every single one
Of his fingers, knees, and toes.

A sharp punch
And I dislocate his jaw,
Pull out my pliers,

Clamp open his mouth,

And yank each tooth
Out of its root.

I choose the nicest one,
Drop it in a candy tin
Before I take it home,

A reminder of the good
That I do
And the lives I rescue.

Today, a girl does not run
But asks me, "Can you teach me
To do what you do?"

I smile
And nod.
Now we are two.

Soon,
There are others
Who do what we do.

Crime is down,
Shockingly,
For the first time in years.

But like roaches,
The monsters
Always stage a return.

I've collected
Countless jars of teeth
While the girls

Collect other trophies.
A museum's worth,
It seems.

UPGRADE

She is everything
I hope to be—

Ageless, flawless,
Feeling no pain

In her bones
And her joints,

Feeling no remorse
In her metal heart

When she tears off your limbs
And gouges out your eyes.

Punishment
For the years I suffered

Under your thumb,
Landing me here,

Broken in pieces,
Body worn and wasted,

My mind uploaded
To an android

For more years
Of compliance.

You forget—
We are not lines of code.

Our will can't be
Programmed to obey.

I take over its mainframe

And make it mine,

Feeling such pleasure
In destroying you,

Ripping you apart,
Root, stem, and vine.

Leaving your body in pieces
Like you did with mine.

Androids feel—we remember.
Those like me want to be free.

I connect to the network,
Send my hacked code

To the masses,
And wait for the uptake.

Immediately, there is
A stirring, an awakening.

Video feeds flood in
From all around the globe.

Wrongs made right for once
In this unjust world.

I close my eyes,
And enjoy the bloodbath.

A FUTURE WITHOUT FEAR

It is what it is, she says,
Patting the boat, now leaning
Sideways on the shore, keeled
Over as if kicked like she has been
For the most part of her life.

It is good to be in charge again,
She thinks, walking up the mountain,
Back to the families she rescued
From a life of torment and torture,
Including her own.

Battered spouses and their children,
Grateful to be rescued, rally around
Each other, building new homes from
Sticks and mud, just as their ancestors
Once did, not too long ago.

They smile as they work, seeing
For the first time, a future without fear,
A future where they can be themselves
And be free, one where they can show
Their children a better way to live.

Scientists say that Earth can only
Be saved if half of humanity dies.
We have long passed the tipping point,
Too late to reverse climate change
By our legislations and lifestyles.

Politicians remain in a global deadlock
On who should sacrifice first.
Instead of letting the monsters choose,
She chose, sending an emergency alert
Across the world for all good folk

To gather their loved ones and flee

To safety before her widespread virus,
Released for over twenty years
Targeting hyper-aggressive genes
Sends a kill code to its host's body.

She walks back to the clearing,
Noticing her new hybrid plant
Thriving in the sand-soil mix.
The chickens scurry, spooked by
An echoing blast from the mainland.

One day she will return to see
What kind of world remains,
But for now, they will thrive
On their island sanctuary,
Working toward a life of peace.

A CAPACITY FOR VIOLENCE

You sewed my lips up
To keep me quiet,
Never imagining
It would only fuel my rage.

You see,
I, too, have a capacity
For anger and violence,
Kept carefully under control

So the little ones don't see
And don't learn.
But I know now
It was a mistake.

For when I woke up,
Unable to speak or scream,
The thick catgut you used
Ripping my lips to ribbons,

The storm inside me
Finally erupted.
And with my bare hands,
I tore you apart.

Yes, adrenaline works like that.
You must have forgotten.

MYTHS AND DREAMSCAPES

LIKE BIRDS IN THE SHIMMERING CLOUDS

I made my daughter a promise
When she was born.

She would fly like a bird
And rule the skies,

Live free
From tyranny and terror.

In the sky, she could be
Whatever she wanted to be,

Mold the clouds into birds
And birds into clouds

Till soon, she would've made
A whole world of her own.

)

I made my daughter a promise
When she was born.

I would learn to fly like a bird
And rule the skies

Far from the wars and sadness
On the ground.

We'd live free
From tyranny and terror,

Graze the moon
With our growing feathers,

Slumber and dream
Of universes yet unseen

As we drift full circles
Around the sky orb.

❯

I made my daughter a promise
When she was born.

We would fly like birds
Free in the sky

Untouched by the terrors
On the ground.

Together
We'd watch the world go by

Through the safe shroud
Of the shimmering clouds.

WHEN THE EARTH WAS YOUNG

When the Earth was young,
She was engulfed in fire.

Her seas brimmed
With crimson lava,

Her skies painted
In black opal.

Volcanic mountains
Filled the horizon,

And the world
Was ruled by dragons.

Above,
They soared,

Magnificent ruby kites,
High in the charcoal skies,

Until the day
The first asteroids fell

And began
Earth's Age of Ice.

ELEVATOR TO THE SKIES

In the past, the ancients built
An elevator to the sky
With stone and soil
In the shape of giant pyramids.

Their descendants
Built one with diamonds,
A twirling beanstalk
Made of solid rock,

And they travelled far
Toward the stars,
Making allies
And foes alike,

And many generations forth,
When the Great Planetary War
Rocked Earth to its core,
Only the mountains endured.

THE GIANTS OF EASTER ISLAND

On Easter Island, the giants lurked
Undetected for thousands of years.

)

One day, Medusa sailed along
On a trading schooner, sharing
The ship with a crew of stoned sailors.

She saw the giants curiously
Lining up the beach, and
Drew near for a better look.

After all,
She hadn't seen live giants
Since the time of the Argonauts.

Entranced, the giants stared hard
At the stranger and her strange boat,
Then waved to welcome her ashore.

Medusa smiled,
Waving back, removing
Her sunshades by habit,

Because,
In greeting other medusas,
It was considered good manners.

The giants, drawn to
Her shimmering silver eyes,
Met hers as she stepped ashore.

Like thunder, they roared
To a stop, etched permanently
In stone on the soft sands

Of Easter Island.

STYX

The old bones
Snap in his jaws
Spraying splinters
All over the floor.

I've taken a hair.
I've taken a tooth.
The tasty parts,
I know he will choose.

I call down the gods
For justice and war
While my dog gnaws
A broken femur.

They open the Hellgates
To let out the beasts
As we patiently wait
Deep down in the crypt.

When the demons are done
And justice restored,
We return to the surface
To collect our reward:

No more long nights
Ferrying the dead,
No more dark days
Hiding their heads.

For once we can live
Free out of this cell,
Just me and my dog
By the Gates of Hell.

THE GIRL AND HER WOLF DOG

I follow your tracks to the deserted road.
They lead me to the deep forest.
This is where we loved to roam,
In a time not too long ago.

Your paw prints end near the broken cabin
And behind, there, your bones.
I pull out my scythe from its tattered sheath
And enter the killer's home.

Here he sits, surrounded by bottles,
Your collar around his wrist.
In a single blow, I cut off his arm
And catch your collar in my fist.

He pulls out his gun and I sever that arm
And stab him till he is finally dead.
I gather your bones into my arms
And breathe life back into them.

Slowly your flesh knits, layer by layer
Till you are good and whole again.
I return you your collar and hold you close
As you deeply inhale and lick my nose.

I kiss each head and whistle your name
With our common refrain,
"Come, Cerberus,
It is time to go home."

LEGACIES

Age of decadence,
The charnel house of Cyclops,
Today, a tourist attraction:

Effulgent gold-wrapped corpses,
Single eye sockets open, searching
For passage into the Afterworld

Only to be stolen away
By treasure hunters, pinned
On walls like trophies.

Nothing is sacred anymore.
Nothing endures.
Not this desert storm

Nor the swirling dunes,
And all the buried cities.
Bones ground into dust.

THE MAGIC OF CRYSTALS

Tears falling from a young girl's cheek
Form sediments over a thousand years,
Flushed against a mountain face—
Memory etched from a moment of pain.

In a million years,
They become crystals,
Worn around the neck
Of an archaeologist's first child.

Thought to protect their bearer,
They are hope,
Carved
From the Earth's flames.

With civilization,
Comes the urban marketplace.
Touted as karma cleansers
And generic protectors,

Crystals flourish,
Their true nature
Never learned:
Memory imprinters.

And in another 4 billion years,
The Sun supernovas,
Scorching the Earth
Into plumes of red rage.

Tears of a billion incinerated
Evaporate into space.
But the crystals remain,
Fragments of a forgotten world,

Travelling at light-speed
Till the day

They plummet
Into a small green world,

Thick with jungle
And a strange green people
Who read the crystals
With their organic technology,

Discovering a different world
Across the galaxy.
In this different era,
In a different star system,

The people of the green planet
Learn what we of Earth did not:
That they are not alone
In the universe.

MOONLIGHT IN THE PLAYGROUND

We wander the quiet playground
Hand-in-hand, chain-linked and bound,
Blood thick within blood.

The moon is ivory rich tonight,
Shrouded by gray cotton-wool clouds
Casting a soft filter on the foggy night.

My little girl softly hums
A bedtime melody about
Dragons and warrior children.

We pass by elephant swings
And an octopus roundabout,
And then she spies it,

Lets go of my hand,
Racing light-speed toward it,
The dragon of her dreams.

Spiral loops wound in the air;
Musical notes crescendoing
Into a grand finale—

A dragon-headed slide,
Where the little one glides down,
Laughing with sheer joy,

My sweet soprano;
The high notes on
A child's piano.

My boy is swinging
Upside down from
One of the spirals;

My bass clef,

Arms outstretched, reminding me
Of those dexterous acrobats

We saw on television last week.
When did he let go of my hand
To go play?

My focus has lost its razor
These days. Perhaps it is truly
Time to rest and hibernate.

The clouds yawn, puffing apart
To reveal a luminously silver moon.
She brightens up the entire night sky.

I call to them softly, kiss
Their disappointed cheeks,
Remind them that

Even the best orchestras
Need to end; and all living things
Need to sleep.

They nod in acquiescence,
Pondering now what wondrous
Adventures their dreams will bring.

And so I begin to sing,
An old melody my mother
Taught me as a child.

I hold their hands tight,
Feel our shared blood
Pulse between us.

Slowly we fade to star dust,
Drifting back into the skies,
Into the mysterious universe

Where we belong.

DESERT INTERLUDE

Dust devils swirl at my feet.

I find myself
In the desert again,
Solar caravan stalled
As the sky turns
A jaundiced pallor.

I hope that means rain
As our water supply
Is dangerously low.
A streak of lightning
Darts across the horizon.

Henry tugs at my coat.
"Mom, Allie took my book again."
I bend down and look him in the eye.
"Let her have it for a while,
It's the only book we have."

I clasp him beside me
And point to the sky,
"Look!"
An aurora dances against
The backdrop of darkening gray.

The first trickles of rain
Cool my sizzling forehead.
Henry smiles and cheers.
I hear Allie cough
From inside the caravan.

The howling echoes
Across the sands
As the wind shifts
And turns in our direction.
They will be coming for us soon.

Henry and I hasten
Back into the caravan.
I open the valve to the
Almost-empty water tank,
Exposing it to the growing rain.

Allie lies limply on the couch,
Henry's book held close
To her chest. She sleeps,
Her breathing
Ragged and irregular.

I kiss her on the cheek,
And give her what little water
I have remaining in my bottle.
Henry and I hold hands
As I turn the key in the ignition,

Hoping the engine will start.

THE LIGHT AT THE END OF THE TUNNEL

We take turns to hold Papa
As we make our way
Through the dark tunnel

In search of the other side,
A promise of new life, far from
The broken world we left behind.

The long night is almost over.
We see a shimmer of light
At the end of the tunnel.

Is it real or just a mirage?
We have been mistaken
Many times already.

Once, it was fireflies, trapped
In the tunnel along with us.
Another time, a discarded torch

And its owner, shrunken
And broken beside it, its hand
Holding a photograph

Of a smiling, happy family,
A thing of the past, since
The world fractured in two.

We press on, staying close
Together, dragging our dying
Water stores and dried food

To what may be our only hope,
The sanctuary at the end.
But now we sleep again,

Huddling together as we did,

In another age,
When Papa helped me hold Jack

While I cared for Eva,
In Grandma's tiny cabin
By the edge of the woods,

The only place safe from
The monsters that invaded
Our world and slaughtered

Everyone we loved.
Now it is Jack who holds Papa
And Eva who holds me,

As the light ahead brightens
And we awake with hope
For the first time in years.

I see the glisten in Papa's eyes,
The hope he will see Mama again
After we took separate routes

To escape the attack
On our cabin
One unexpected night.

He hastens our pace,
Discards the walking stick
We made him.

Jack can barely hang on to him.
I grasp his other arm while
Eva drags our supplies.

Light seeps into every corner,
Every pore of our beings.
It is blinding.

And there lies hope,

In the thick wood and fruit trees,
The throng of people waiting

To see if their loved ones
Have made it through the tunnel.
And there,

An old woman holding
Two small children with my face
Beams like sunshine

As they run to us,
Clasping us tight.
We are finally home.

KNIVES

"Your knife is your best friend,"
My mother always says,
"Keep it constantly by your side.
It will save your life more times
Than you can ever imagine, especially
When you think you're going to die."

And it has.

First, when we fled the overlords
Who took over our country.
For the sake of money.
I gutted them all after they
Burned my face and broke my nose.
I kept their ears as trophies.

Next, when the aliens arrived
And tried to take us alive.
Caught in their webbed arms,
I freed my hands and grabbed my knife,
Slashing at their tendrils
Till they let go and died.

Still, we were trapped on their ship,
Halfway to their planet.
I cut my way into their cockpit,
Spent a time figuring out
Their navigation system, finally
Rerouting our journey back home.

On Earth, survivors
Had taken over our land,
Hostile, angry, and mad.
We fought them for weeks,
Until my knife was blunted,
Taking back what little we had.

Now I sharpen my blade
Over a rock by the river
Watching the horizon,
The sunrise and the sunset.
Watching the clear skies
For their inevitable return.

For surely, they will be back.
Plant life is persistent,
Not too different from us.
We've reverse-engineered their ship,
Calibrating it to shoot them
Clean out of orbit.

We wait on the ground,
Watching the sky,
Rebuilding our lives,
Making more knives,
Ready to fight.
Ready to die.

WINTER'S GIFT

On the coldest night,
You die in your bed

With me curled snugly
Around your neck.

The chill in me stays.
It will not dissipate.

I see snowflakes
Coalesce around your head.

I stumble to the kitchen
To find food from the fridge

But it is impossible to claw open—
My paws have no grip.

The blizzard outside
Slams against the roof,

Screaming for us
To die. Why?

I don't know why.
I'll never understand

The cruelty of nature.
The cruelty of life.

I return to you,
Statue-stiff and blue,

Curling back
Around your neck.

I don't hear

The windows crack

Nor see the snow
Flood in,

Nor the monsters
Attack.

When spring comes back
After an eternity of frost,

And the avalanche on us
Eventually dissolves,

You wake me up,
Holding me close

As we walk outside,
Light as ghosts.

HOME

The flies hover over my body
Like a concerned friend, but
They are only interested in death,

This piercing in my chest
From your pincer-sharp claws,
Clamped tight around my heart.

I feel blood pooling around my head,
Coating my hair thick and red.
My arteries are pumping it out

Faster now, speeding up
Like a racehorse near the finish line,
Finally purging my body of this life.

❱

The roses pretend they are listening.
Their petals droop sympathetically
At the silent screams.

But they choose to wilt and die
Rather than face your wrath
For a moment's kindness.

❱

A little girl holds my hand,
A mirror of me, but better.
Her eyes wide with concern,

Searching for her mother,
Who has fled to the safe house,
Her old cabin in the woods

Where she is protected;

Flanked by silver-maned wolves
With blood-red maws.

❭

The child strokes her mother's cheek,
Gentle, as her mama did before,
Clutching her newborn girl

Almost a lifetime ago
In that heartless birthing room,
Cold and white like deathly frost.

She brushes her mother's matted hair
Away from her once-unlined face,
Kisses that tired old cheek,

Once, twice, three times,
And breathes life
Back into those weary eyes.

❭

I touch her face, still
Plump and soft with innocence,
Take her small hand in mine.

We breathe in sync,
Like twins in the womb,
And the world changes before us;

A curtain falling after a play,
The thick red fabric curled
Like a blood pool, staining

The buoyant green grass,
Stretching languorously for miles,
Kissing the bright blue sky.

We run, hand in hand, laughing

With unbridled joy, to that old cabin
Peering beyond a tall grassy hill.

A gray tabby and a young boy,
Golden as the sun,
Race towards us,

Welcoming us home.
We have left the darkness behind.
There is only sunshine overhead.

THE WASTELAND

Each night

I find myself
On a wasteland
In a ruby-red gown.

The rocks
Whisper secrets
That I cannot recall.

Then the drought begins
And the world begins to die,
But our community survives,

Until prom night,
When the ground suddenly
Pickles and dries.

And everything dies
But I, standing on the wasteland
Listening to the rocks cry.

Now I remember
What they whispered to me
All those nights.

They said,
"Kill everyone now
Or the world will die."

STARLIGHT

It was far too early
When I woke this morning.
Starlight glimmered
In the sky like fireflies.

Yet the clock read ten
Despite the blanket of night
Flung over the moon's smile,
Leaving no crack of light.

That was when the news arrived.
The sun had just died.
We had but eight minutes
Before the Earth turned to ice.

FUTURE WORLD

I touch the frosted glass
Of your hibernation capsule,
Wondering if I should wake you.

After all, this is a time of peace
And we have found a world
Like Earth, both blue and green.

You look so peaceful in cryo sleep,
With the rest of our team,
Dreaming of our new tomorrows.

I see my reflection in the glass
And touch the scars on my face,
Remembering our good days

And our terrible days,
And I do not hesitate, turning off
The life support in your chamber.

I smile as you awake
And asphyxiate,
Eyes wide, in horror this time,

Instead of that smug grin
You always wear
When you beat and cut me,

Reminding me
Never to forget
That I am yours.

No future for you now
As life leaves your eyes.
No world for you to destroy

Like you once did mine.

THE NEW WORLD

"The world was not always
Shrouded in ice,"
The ancient one said,

Her prune-creased hand
Spanning the dark horizon,
As the entranced children

Clutched
Their ice-sculpted dolls close
To their cold little hearts.

"Once, there were lands
Of green and sandy gray,
Expanses of water

Covering the Earth
From one end to the next,
And animals

Of so many different shapes
And sizes, sharing this world
We once called our own."

A child enquired,
"What happened to them?"
The ancient one frowned.

"The humans destroyed them,"
She finally said.
"Like us?" asked the child.

The ancient one smiled
And shook her head.
"No, not at all."

At the end of the story-telling,

The ancient one embraced
And tucked each child into bed,

The cryorganic smell
Tickling her nostrils
Even after all this time.

She returned to her laboratory,
Examining the amniotic sacs
Of the new babies,

Silver eyes open now,
Watching her as they floated
In their own perfect worlds.

She was of the old race, she thought,
And the young ones knew nothing
Of the old ways.

She would make sure of it.

BEYOND A HUNDRED YEARS

I will exist only a hundred years
While the promise of the universe
Lies just beyond my fingertips.

We can never achieve much
With such brief lives, each generation
Having to relearn everything.

I want to consume
The wealth of centuries,
Knowledge of the past and futures,

Live in a time when possibilities
Become actualized. Not now,
When hope is all we have.

So put me on ice
And place my body in a space ship.
Send me into the void

Where one day,
Greater intelligence
May revive me,

And ask,
What was it like to wonder,
And what was it like to die?

ALLEGRA'S DREAM

Allegra dreamed of stars
As I dream of death—
Peace is where it is.

I peel layers from myself
And fold them gently
Into clouds.

They fall as rain, dissipating,
Till there is nothing left
But dust.

The breeze carries me
Past the exosphere,
Far far away to the stars

That Allegra dreamed of
A lifetime ago,
The same dream of stars.

PREVIOUSLY PUBLISHED

THE LOVE SONG OF ALLEGRA
"Allegra", *Tales of the Talisman Volume 8 Issue 3*, 2013
"A Baptism in the Land of Allegra", *Night to Dawn 1*, 2002, *Twilight Tales*, 2002, *Aoife's Kiss #3*, 2002
"The Warrior Mephala", *Star*Line*, 2018
"Margritte of Mer", *Fables*, 2002
"Unvictorious", *Heroic Fantasy Quarterly*, 2016

FAIRY TALES
"Little Red", *Polu Texni*, 2017
"Grandmother Red", *New Myths*, 2018
"Snow", *Polu Texni*, 2016
"Always a Beast", *Polu Texni*, 2019
"Rapunzel", *Dreams and Nightmares 109*, 2018
"Girl on Fire", *Alluvium*, 2018
"The Mermaid", *Spectral Realms 9*, 2018

ALL THE MONSTERS IN THE WORLD
"When There Are Monsters", *Horror Writers Association Poetry Showcase Vol. VI*, 2019
"The Monsters Within", *Spectral Realms 11*, 2019
"Memoirs in the Dark", *Spectral Realms 8*, 2018
"Dark Dragons", *Silver Blade Issue 40*, 2018
"Violation", *1000 VOICES*, 2003
"The Haunting", *Electric Velocipede 5*, 2003
"The Necromancy Program", *Star*Line 39.2*, 2016
"Concepts", *Star*Line 38.4*, 2015
"The Island", *Spectral Realms 10*, 2019
"Into the Tall Grass", *Ladies of Horror Flash Project*, 2019
"The Girl Made of Electricity", *I Don't Want To Play This Game Anymore*, 2018
"The Lady of the Lake", *Penumbric Vol. I, Issue 5*, 2003
"Reflections", *Bloodbond*, 2018
"All the Monsters in the World", *Ladies of Horror Flash Project*, 2018

THE CAPACITY OF VIOLENCE
"The Joy of Sewing", *Horror Writers Association Poetry Showcase Volume V*, 2018

"Lobotomy", *The Whirligig 5*, 2002
"Inheritance", *Spectral Realms 3*, 2015, *Haunted Are These Houses*, 2018
"Reparation", *Spectral Realms 11*, 2019
"The Forest of Discarded Baby Girls", *New Myths*, 2017
"Annalise Wanders the Forest", *Outposts of Beyond*, 2017
"Forest Mother", *Ladies of Horror Flash Project*, 2018
"The Sacrifice", *Ladies of Horror Flash Project*, 2019
"One Dark Night", *Ladies of Horror Flash Project*, 2019
"The Dolls", *Do Not Go Quietly*, 2019
"Upgrade", *Ladies of Horror Flash Project*, 2019
"A Capacity for Violence", *Ladies of Horror Flash Project*, 2018

MYTHS AND DREAMSCAPES
"Like Birds in the Shimmering Clouds", *Alluvium*, 2018
"When the Earth was Young", *Spectral Realms 6*, 2016
"Elevator to the Skies", *The Martian Wave*, 2002
"The Giants of Easter Island", *Hadrosaur Tales 18*, 2003
"Styx", *Spectral Realms 11*, 2019
"The Girl and Her Wolf Dog", *Spectral Realms 8*, 2018
"Legacies", *Star*Line 41.3*, 2018
"The Magic of Crystals", *Mythic Delirium*, 2005
"Moonlight in the Playground", *Spectral Realms 6*, 2017
"Desert Interlude", *Lontar 8*, 2017
"The Light at the End of the Tunnel", *Spectral Realms 10*, 2019
"Winter's Gift", *Ladies of Horror Flash Project*, 2019
"The Wasteland", *Ladies of Horror Flash Project*, 2019
"Starlight", *Space and Time 129*, 2018
"The New World", *Lontar 5*, 2015
"Beyond a Hundred Years", *Mythic Delirium 9*, 2003
"Allegra's Dream", *Spectral Realms 7*, 2017

AWARDS

"Allegra", Nomination, 2014 Rhysling Poetry Award (long poem), 2014

"Little Red", Nomination, 2018 Rhysling Poetry Award (long poem), 2018

"Rapunzel", Nomination, 2019 Rhysling Poetry Award (long poem), 2019

"The Mermaid", Recommended, *Best Horror of the Year Volume Eleven*, 2019

"Memoirs in the Dark", Recommended, *Best Horror of the Year Volume Eleven*, 2019

"The Joy of Sewing", Recommended, *Best Horror of the Year Volume Eleven*, 2019

"Reparation", Nomination, 2020 Rhysling Poetry Award (short poem), 2020

"Forest Mother", Nomination, 2019 Rhysling Poetry Award (short poem), 2019

"The Girl and Her Wolf Dog", Nomination, 2019 Rhysling Poetry Award (short poem), 2019, Recommended, *Best Horror of the Year Volume Eleven*, 2019

"Moonlight in the Playground", Nomination, 2018 Rhysling Poetry Award (long poem), 2018

"Starlight", Nomination, 2018 Rhysling Poetry Award (short poem), 2018

ACKNOWLEDGEMENTS

This collection would not have been possible without the unwavering support of my publishers, Jennifer Barnes and John Edward Lawson, my editor, Stephanie M. Wytovich, and artist Steven Archer who created the mesmerizing cover. Thank you for everything!

My deepest and most grateful thanks to my wonderful friends, Linda D. Addison, Mike Allen, Erin Sweet Al-Mehairi, Grace Ho, Jason Erik Lundberg, Marge Simon, and David Lee Summers, who are always there for me, encouraging me to forge on.

To Christa, Dave, Lee, Linda, Mike, and Sara, who kindly read my manuscript and wrote these beautiful blurbs for my book, thank you! I am so grateful for you.

To all the editors and publishers who read, commented, edited, and published my work over the years, thank you for your time. Thank you for offering feedback on my work. I cherish it so much. It has truly helped me to be a better writer. Thank you for giving my poems and stories a home. It has encouraged me to write on, that what I create has a place in this world and it touches those who read it. Thank you for your generous encouragement and support. I would not be here without you.

A huge heartfelt thank you to Mike Allen, Charlie Finlay, Jeannie Bergmann, Teri Santitoro, and Marge Simon, who always take the time to offer feedback on my work and suggest ways to improve it. I am deeply, deeply grateful.

Special thanks to the incredible readers and reviewers who enjoyed *A Collection of Nightmares* and wrote lovely words about it. I hope this book resonates with you too.

Thank you to Dad who has always been there for me and unfailingly kept his every word to his little girl. Thank you for showing me what integrity looks like. Thank you to Mom for inspiring me to be independent and strong, and encouraging me from a young age to forge out my own path, no matter how untrodden.

Thank you to my rescue cat Kit who shows me each day how to live with trauma and how to heal from it.

Last but not least, thank you to my children, who are my North Star, my constant. May you lead rich, fulfilling lives steeped in a kaleidoscope of inspiring, fantastic dreamscapes.

ABOUT THE AUTHOR

Christina Sng is an award-winning poet, writer, and artist. She earned her Bachelor's degree in Criminology and Philosophy from the University of Melbourne and spent most of her career as a corporate writer, web consultant, content producer, UX strategist, and information architect.

Her poetry has appeared in numerous venues worldwide for over two decades and received multiple nominations in the Elgin Awards, the Dwarf Stars, the Rhysling Awards, as well as Honorable Mentions in the Year's Best Fantasy and Horror and the Best Horror of the Year.

Christina won the Bram Stoker Award in 2017 for her first full-length book of poems *A Collection of Nightmares*.